# Botallack O'Clock

## By Eddie Elks

**Published by Playdead Press 2013**



A CIP catalogue record for this book is available from the British Library.

ISBN 978-0-9576077-4-3



**Playdead Press**
**www.playdeadpress.com**

***Botallack O'Clock*** premiered at the Half Moon, Herne Hill in August 2011. It then went on to play at the Edinburgh Festival 2012 and transferred to the 59E59 Theaters, New York as part of the annual Brits Off Broadway Season 2013.

CAST

Half Moon, Herne Hill – 11th – 27th August 2011

| | |
|---|---|
| ROGER | Dan Frost |
| RADIO/ BEAR | Mark Knightley |

Gilded Balloon, Edinburgh Festival – 1st – 27th August 2012

| | |
|---|---|
| ROGER | Dan Frost |
| RADIO/ BEAR | Rhys King |

59E59 Theaters, New York – May 20th – June 9th 2013

| | |
|---|---|
| ROGER | Dan Frost |
| RADIO/ BEAR | Rhys King |

Written and Directed by Eddie Elks

# third man theatre

Third Man Theatre is an award winning theatre company based in London and Cornwall that specialises in new writing. Since forming in 2007, Third Man Theatre have toured extensively throughout the UK performing at various venues and festivals.

Previous shows include STALAG HAPPY by Eddie Elks and Dan Frost (Spirit of the Fringe Award 2009), THE LINE BETWEEN by Dan Frost and Mark Knightley and THE ONE THAT GOT AWAY devised by Third Man.

REVIEWS for BOTALLACK O'CLOCK

**Time Out – Critics' Choice**

*****

"Dazzlingly eloquent yet always just beyond sense...
Botallack O'Clock is a stunning miniature; surprising,
profound and very very funny..."

NOMINATED: Best Fringe Play 2011 Time Out

**Edfringe Review – EDITOR'S PICK**

*****

"Comic, insightful, and unmissable!"

**Exeunt Magazine – EDITOR'S PICK**

****

"Botallack O'Clock is a powerful success."

**one4review**

****

"Bitingly funny... wildly chaotic..."

**a younger theatre**

****

"A strange, surreal experience..."

**Broadway Baby**

****

"a rare combination of funny and thought-provoking."

**Bristol Evening News**

9/10

"a powerful journey through a troubled mind."

## ROGER HILTON CBE

Roger Hilton's extraordinary career began as a figurative artist, yet in the 1950s he became involved in the most important school of British abstraction, which emerged from St Ives, Cornwall. This included the artists Sir Ben Nicholson, Peter Lanyon, Sir Patrick Heron, Dame Barbara Hepworth and Sir Terry Frost. Roger's painting went in and out of figuration and abstraction during his final years in the 1970s, when his work became known for its colourful, fresh qualities alongside its humour, rudeness and the poignancy of an artist struggling with deteriorating health.

Throughout this period, Hilton's productivity increased dramatically, mainly during the night. He produced a huge body of work, using poster paint on paper, a shift from his earlier oil paintings. As well as these gouaches, he wrote many letters to Rose, published collectively in *The Night Letters*. Along with interviews, recordings and the paintings themselves, these letters have provided the inspiration, material and even the soundtrack (Roger's list of Desert Island Discs) for *Botallack O'Clock*. They give an incredible insight into Roger's character, revealing his intelligence, passion and dedication.

After his death, several offers were made to the family to dramatize Roger's story on film, one with the possibility of having John Hurt in the title role. These were all declined, mainly due to the fact that Roger had two young sons.

Thirty – five years on, the family granted Third Man Theatre permission to bring his story to the stage, which also coincided with what would have been Roger's 100th year.

## WRITER'S NOTE

Everyone who knew or has met, or has even just heard of Roger Hilton seems to have a story about him, such is his reputation. I first heard of him whilst in Cornwall researching Stalag Happy in 2007. His name kept popping up in books, interviews and conversations, always connected with an entertaining, intriguing and often shocking story. When I returned to London I bought one of Roger's biographies and began to realise the dramatic potential of his story.

Two years later Rose Hilton, Roger's widow, came to see Stalag Happy at the St Ives Arts Club. We met after the show and spoke about Roger and his friendship with Sir Terry Frost – upon whose life Stalag Happy is based.

I returned to London and dusted off the biography. I contacted Rose asking permission to write about Roger. I was extremely pleased when a letter came back granting her consent – and coincidently it happened to be Roger's centenary year.

Over the next 8 months and several trips down to Cornwall to stay with Rose, Botallack O'Clock evolved – the title coming from the Sydney Graham poem *"The Lines on Roger Hilton's Watch"*. Throughout the whole experience I tried to follow Roger's artistic instructions. A large amount of the text has come directly from Roger's letters and interviews. It was if Roger guided – sometimes ordered – me through it all! My main aim was to find a fitting way to give life to such witty, insightful and inspiring words and also reflect Roger's personality and paintings within style of the piece. In a letter to his mother, whilst serving in WWII, Roger wondered whether one day his life would be made into a story. I hope he would have approved. If nothing else, Roger finally got to appear on Desert Island Discs (well sort of, you know!).

ACKNOWLEDGEMENTS

Special thanks to: Rose Hilton, Bo Hilton, Ronnie Duncan, Anthony, Linda and Luke Frost, Ken McClymont, Lara Rossi, David Thomson, Dudley Sutton, Steve Frost, Janet Prince, Karen Koren, Stewart Lee, Hannah, Lucy and Zannah at PilotLight Theatre, The Half Moon in Herne Hill, Bob and Louise at Advanced Graphics London, Georgia Stoneman at Stoneman Gallery, Bob Devereux, The St.Ives Arts Club, Timothy Bond, Charlie and Ros Forbes-Adams, Caroline Wiseman, Francis Carnwarth CBE, Paul Jellis, Danny Clancy, The Archive of Modern Conflict, Jonathan Clark Gallery, Beaux Arts Gallery, Messums Gallery, Anthony, Sandra and Charles Holmes, George and Elspeth Elks.

*For Roger and Rose*

*Botallack Moor, Cornwall – 1975*

*Roger Hilton's cottage – a ground floor room.*

*Darkness*

*Roger lies on his bed – a single mattress on top of a legless bed base. There is a small table in front of the bed covered in paints, brushes, a water jar, paper, ashtrays, cigarettes, two whisky bottles, an apple and a small bell. A RADIO sits on a small stool next to the bed. The floor is covered in mess – paint, clothes, jars, paper, food, bottles. A light hangs above the bed – attached to a pulley allowing it to be risen and lowered. A wardrobe stands upstage left leading to the backstage area and there is a low rope barrier across front of stage. The walls are flats made from canvas. Paintings hang on the walls drying.*

*Extract from "The Lines in Roger Hilton's Watch"*
*by W.S.Graham – read by W.S.Graham*

VO Tell me the time. The time

Is Botallack O'Clock.

This is the dead of night.

He switches the light on

To find a cigarette

And pours himself a Teachers.

He picks me up and holds me

Near his lonely face

To see my hands. He thinks

He is not being watched.

*RH turns on hanging light above his head*

*Back to audience*

*A ticking clock is heard*

*He pours a whisky*

*Lights a cigarette*

*Drinks*

*Looks at pocket watch*

*Clock ticks*

*He drinks and smokes*

*He rolls over and lies on his back*

*He smokes*

*Clock ticks*

*Without looking he picks up a paint brush from the floor. He taps it on empty whisky bottle. Then on to water jar and bottle. Cacophony of tapping/ ticking. Builds louder and louder until…*

SILENCE

*He lifts himself on to his side*

*The hanging light slowly brightens*

*He pulls his legs off the bed – eventually into sitting*

*He puts on his glasses*

*He slowly looks up*

*He looks out*

*He pours himself a whisky and lights a cigarette*

*He looks at his watch – listens to it – shakes it – listens again*

*He gathers painting equipment*

*Drinks*

*He turns on RADIO*

*White noise crackles*

*He tunes the RADIO – white noise/ voices/ music*

*Turns off RADIO*

*Turns on RADIO – white noise*

*Turns off RADIO*

*Turns on RADIO – white noise*

*He hits RADIO with brush*

*And again*

*And again*

*Turns off RADIO*

*RH waves brush over radio*

*He taps the RADIO three times*

*He slowly goes to turn on RADIO*

*He turns on RADIO – white noise*

*He hits RADIO*

*White noise stops*

*He prepares his painting equipment*

*He looks out at audience*

*He paints*

*He drinks*

*He smokes*

RH This is the worst time of the night.

3 till 4.

The evening long gone – the morning nowhere in sight.

No hopes of dawn. No birdsong.

A suspended hour.

Suspension.

Hanging.

Swinging.

*BEAT*

Balls.

*Looks at his watch.*

Everyone else is asleep.

Not me. Not you.

Not yet.

*Back to the painting*

Don't begin until you know what to do.

Do nothing.

*BEAT*

In my beginning is my end...

No not a poem. Don't begin with a poem for Christ's sake.

Wait for it. If you don't get a clear message – do nothing.

Do nothing.

*BEAT*

Patience is a virtue

Possess it if you can

Find it in a woman

But never in a man.

*BEAT*

Balls.

Sing a song of sixpence a pocket full of rye,

Four and twenty blackbirds baked in a pie,

When the pie was open the birds began to sing,

Wasn't that a dainty dish to place before the king?

*BEAT*

A man's subconscious self is not the ideal companion.

It lurks for the greater part of his life in some dark den of its own, hidden away. Then it emerges only to taunt and deride and increase the misery of a miserable hour.

Don't force yourself to do something. It either happens or it doesn't.

It either happens or it doesn't.

*BEAT*

It doesn't.

Well I'm not going to sing again.

This isn't the London Palladium.

Do you want a song and dance?

Not on my watch.

Don't begin until you know what to do.

Do nothing.

*BEAT*

Well you have to do something.

I can't just sit here like some old lemon.

Well?

Rely on your instinct.

No?

Tis a naughty night to swim in...

No?

Sod it then.

*He arranges his paints*

Blue, green, black...

Where's the red? Where's the red?

*He searches for the red paint*

*He sees red paint on the floor at the other end of the bed*

*He stretches for it – more and more…*

*He knocks paint out of his reach*

*Collapses into bed*

Bugger it.

Might just lie here for a while... Quite nice.

*BEAT*

In through the cage of words the people

Stared at the beast to have a laugh.

There was no beast but that great beast

Will bite their noses off.

*White noise crackles from RADIO*

*RADIO glows with light*

*Hanging light flickers*

*From the white noise comes Sleepy Lagoon (Desert Island Discs Theme Tune)*

*The white noise subsides leaving just the music playing*

*RADIO light and hanging light stop flickering*

RADIO Welcome to Desert Island Discs. The programme where each week our castaway chooses the soundtrack to their life. This week's castaway needs no introduction. He is one of the country's most revered artists – he is of course...

*Music stops*

Roger Hilton.

*RH looks up*

Good evening.

*BEAT*

Good evening.

*BEAT*

Hello.

Hello?

RH Hello?

RADIO Good evening.

*BEAT*

RH Me?

RADIO You.

RH Me?

RADIO You. Yes you.

RH Well bloody hell...

| | |
|---|---|
| RADIO | Hello Roger. |
| RH | Well hello. |
| RADIO | Pleasure to have you on the show. |
| RH | Well – it's about bloody time – ten years I've been waiting. |
| RADIO | You're looking well. |
| RH | So are you. |
| RADIO | Busy? |
| RH | Run off my feet. |
| RADIO | Aren't we all. |
| RH | Yes, yes, yes. |
| RADIO | Would you like a drink? |
| RH | Yes, good idea – thank you very much. |

*He pours himself a drink*

Your health.

*Drinks*

| | |
|---|---|
| RH | Well. |
| RADIO | Well. |
| RH | So. |
| RADIO | So? |

RH | Shouldn't you ask me a question or something?
--- | ---

| | |
|---|---|
| RH | Shouldn't you ask me a question or something? |
| RADIO | Yes. |
| RH | Go on then. Ask me a question. |
| RADIO | What shall I ask you? |
| RH | I don't know. What do they normally say? Ask me how life is or something? |
| RADIO | How's life Roger? |
| RH | Bloody awful. |
| | I paint in bed. |
| | I move the bed to there and there. |
| | Sometimes there |
| | *BEAT* |
| | Or there. |
| | I have been forced to lean on my left side so I've been painting with my right hand. |
| | A good thing perhaps as I have become too accomplished with my left. |
| | Everyone else is asleep. |
| | Not me. |
| | Not you. |

| | |
|---|---|
| RADIO | Not yet. |
| RH | No, not yet. |
| | Well? |
| RADIO | Yes? |
| RH | Question. |
| RADIO | Would you like some roast duck? |
| RH | I beg your pardon. |
| RADIO | How about some roast pheasant? |
| RH | What? |
| RADIO | Grouse? |
| RH | No. |
| RADIO | Ptmaigan? |
| RH | Listen... |
| RADIO | Quail? |
| RH | Look! |
| RADIO | Partridge? |

*RH hits RADIO – RADIO flashes*

| | |
|---|---|
| RH | What's wrong with you? |
| | Christ – have you done this before? |

RADIO Well...

RH Well?

RADIO No.

RH This is a bloody shambles.

Ask me what paint I use or something...

RADIO What paint do you use?

RH Unbelievable.

Well one comes up through the orange peel, the mackerel, the shrimps, the children, the nappies, the motor cars, to a new calm – poster paint on paper.

They prove to be very good. My son was given them for Christmas and I started using them, you know. They dry very quickly. And they're cheap – but they won't fade. I checked.

I'm painting between three to five gouaches a day, well night. I don't sleep so well.

Whilst I have my food, things get dropped on the paper. Milk bottles get upset, spaghetti, sweet corn and cats...

I tidy up the mess with a few simple strokes.

It's true, as my wife points out, that I no longer have any balls, but I get from painting a kind of soulagement, a harmony akin to music, although I am against too much music for painters.

| | |
|---|---|
| RADIO | I have a question. |
| RH | Go on. |
| RADIO | Why did you become an abstract artist? |
| RH | That's better. |
| RADIO | Thank you very much. |
| RH | Don't get too cocky. |
| RADIO | Of course not. |
| RH | Well, the direct imitation of life or nature can't express the complex situation in which we exist. It can't. |

Human kind cannot bear very much reality.

Correct.

The artist's range is omnivorous – he takes in everything.

But don't try to understand everything. Don't try to *understand*,

You won't find the answers.

Look.

RADIO Look.

RH Feel.

RADIO Feel.

RH Watch.

RADIO Tick tock.

RH You see, we think in *words*. And that's the problem. One tries to put everything into words. You can't understand a picture in *words*.

You see painting is a personal thing, like a shit or a fuck. It's what it means to *you*. That's what I believed in so that's what I did. I was being true to myself.

Faith and truth are everything.

Good.

You know?

*BEAT*

Are you there?

*RADIO snores*

Are you listening?

*RADIO snores*

*RH hits RADIO – RADIO flashes*

RADIO Black socks they never get dirty...

RH What?

Listen you little wretch – don't you shnod off!

RADIO It's very late. My batteries / are...

RH Bollocks and the same to you.

I know what time it is.

*RH taps RADIO - flashes*

RADIO Ow, ow, owww.

*RH looks at watch.*

RH Well, what next?

RADIO I'm not sure.

RH You're not very good at this are you?

RADIO It's my first time.

RH What about a song or something?

RADIO Yes music – of course.

RH There you go.

*BEAT*

RADIO What shall we do with a drunken sailor,

What shall we do with a drunken sailor,

RH No you, not you, not you!

RADIO What shall we do with a drunken sailor...

*RH hits RADIO – flashes*

*RADIO stops singing*

RH I'm going to have to get you fixed.

Now, are you listening?

RADIO All aboard.

RH Good.

My first choice is...

What is my first choice?

*RH looks under table for his list - finds it*

My first choice is... ah yes... good. My first choice is Artur Schnabel playing Beethoven. Beautiful. Sonata 8. It's good, very good.

*Music – Beethoven; Sonata 8 in C Minor Op. 13 "Pathetique"*

*Deep blue lights slowly fade up on to the walls*

*He lights cigarette*

*He listens*

I don't think one could possibly survive in their solitude without Beethoven.

*After a time*

Don't throw yourself on to your canvas – look for a long time at your model!

I hope you're listening.

*BEAT*

For a long time.

*He notices his water jar*

*He holds up water jar*

Bloody cat.

It drinks my paint water.

Thirsty bloody beast.

*He rings bell*

*He looks at the jar*

I read yesterday of an alcoholic, who refused treatment, who got in to a plane at Biggin Hill. Nothing strange was noticed – then the plane was seen performing aerobatics over the rooftops and finally crashed in to a field.

In the wreckage they found an empty bottle of vodka and a corpse.

*BEAT*

Bloody cat.

It maddens me.

I found it on the table demolishing the cheese.

The cheese for god's sake!

Not a mouse! A bloody cat!

*He rings bell*

Are you a man or a mouse?

RADIO A wife or a louse?!

*RH hits RADIO – flashes*

*Music stops – Lights change*

*He looks at a painting hanging on the wall*

A lady once said to me. "That's nice – did Fergus do it?"

*BEAT*

Fergus is my son.

Aged 8.

*RADIO laughs and glows*

Quiet you.

Children's art is often charming and one can borrow from it. But the difference is that children are essentially *realists*, whereas a mature painter is not.

*He looks at picture*

No, I don't really like looking at them once they're off the production line. I prefer to get on with the next one.

When we come to select, it's a painful process.

Pictures are *like* children, it's difficult to see them depart.

*BEAT*

Question.

RADIO Urm...

RH For god's sake – luxury item, luxury item.

RADIO Yes – now you are allowed one luxury item on your desert island. / What would you...

RH Hammer – nails – wood.

RADIO That's three items.

RH Together they would make *one* boat.

RADIO You're not allowed to do that.

RH Why not?

| | |
|---|---|
| RADIO | You can't escape. |
| RH | Balls. |
| | Listen I make the rules around here. |
| RADIO | And I'm asking the questions. |
| RH | And I'm giving the answers. |
| | And the answers are all correct. |
| RADIO | That's show business! |
| RH | No business like it. |
| | Question. |
| RADIO | Other than painting, what else do you like to do? |
| RH | Well, I don't think a man should have too many play things or distractions. There should be only one distraction. His work, his wife, his children. |
| | In that order. |
| | Discipline for any artist is essential. |
| | Question. |
| RADIO | Who is your greatest influence? |
| RH | My dog, Wogs. Taught me everything I know. It's a damn fine dog. |
| | Next. |

| | |
|---|---|
| RADIO | What would you have been if you had not been an artist? |
| RH | A radio engineer. |
| | Next. |
| RADIO | Have you a lewd mind? |
| RH | What the hell has it got to do with you? |
| | And yes, I do. |
| | Next. |
| RADIO | Where you a happy child? |
| RH | Next. |
| RADIO | Is't not the king? |
| RH | Ay, every inch a king – a Botallack Monster King. |
| | Another. |
| RADIO | How many surrealists does it take to change a light bulb? |
| RH | Two. One to hold the bear and the other to fill the bathtub with brightly coloured jelly. |
| | Another. |
| RADIO | I'm running out of questions. |
| RH | Come on, think, think, think. |

| | |
|---|---|
| RADIO | What question shall I ask? |
| RH | Well not that one. |
| RADIO | Well what one? |
| RH | A different one. |
| RADIO | Can the river run red? |
| RH | Yes. Next! |
| RADIO | Does the dark desert dance? |
| RH | Yes. Next! |
| RADIO | Are the seven seas scarlet? |
| RH | Yes. Next! |
| RADIO | Is the primrose path purple? |
| RH | Yes! The primrose path is purple. The primrose path is purple! |

*RADIO exhales*

*RH taps on water jar*

That way madness lies, let's shun that.

Words.

*Words.*

Words and art don't go together.

I'd like another song.

*RADIO sings*

RADIO — Oh Danny Boy, the pipes the pipes are calling...

RH — For God's sake.

*RH hits RADIO – flashes*

I would like Beggars Opera – very good. They sing and dance, you know.

*Music – Beggars Opera; A Fox May Steal Your Hens*

Lovely stuff, really lovely.

*RH listens*

*White light fades up on walls*

*He picks up apple from the table*

*Searches for another*

*Music swells*

*Looks up*

*Music stops – Lights change*

She's pinched the more interesting of my two apples.

*He rings bell*

14 years with one wife, 14 years with this one...

*He rings bell*

Je ne' regret rien.

The rotter.

*He throws the apple on to floor*

*Picks up a letter – begins to add to it*

RADIO What's that?

RH It's a letter to my wife.

RADIO Where is she?

RH Up stairs.

*RH reads*

Start here.

Bad day for quarrels yesterday. Let's start another. Who were you talking to all that time in the lane, outside the door when you got back? I'm asking you who it was and don't say you can't remember and it was definitely a man.

Get some more ham.

And beetroot.

Most things damage the stomach, you see.

Egg cups, hankies, sheets.

No more asparagus – revolting.

More whisky.

Spaghetti. Ravioli. Potatoes. Butter. Spring onions. Garlic. Spinach.

*RH writes*

Apples.

*RH hits RADIO – flashes*

Batteries.

It's all my fault. I am a shit.

Thank you.

*He puts letter down*

RADIO Question?

RH Question.

RADIO I have a question.

RH Go for it.

RADIO Do you paint portraits?

RH Good one.

RADIO Thank you.

RH Yes, I can paint portraits. I mean fuck portraits, but yes I can paint them. People need a pretty portrait for them to believe you can paint.

Proof.

I painted a great many portraits. God knows where they all are. I haven't the faintest clue where they've gone. They seem to have disappeared. I had a show at the Bloomsbury Gallery, which is now extinct, in I think '36 – there was a very good portrait of my sister when about 17 and I mean it really looked nice, you know?

God knows where it's gone. It's a mystery to me.

Somebody told me I burnt them all.

I don't believe it. They were too good to burn.

They do allow one to take in the eyes – follow you around. A glimpse through the crack, the character, the soul, you know.

Preserved.

Pickled in paint.

No, it's a shame they're gone. People would like to see that you could actually do portraits.

But fuck portraits.

RADIO Fuck portraits.

RH Yes – fuck them.

RADIO Fuck ‘em.

RH Fuck ‘em!

RADIO Fuck ‘em!

RH Fuck ‘em!

RADIO Fuck ‘em!

RH There was one of a girl at the Academie. A model. I spent a long time over it. Which was quite good – very good I think. I was rather keen on her. Made it easier, you know.

Think her name was May.

Yes May. Or was it?

No it was May.

The models in Paris, you know.

Long time ago now.

RADIO Tell me about Paris.

*Music – Weber; Invitation to the Dance*

RH Paris?

God I loved Paris. Marvellous Paris.

It’s not the same now... though I suppose everybody says that.

|  |  |
|---|---|
|  | I studied there. I was in my early twenties. Great days. |
| RADIO | Where did you live? |
| RH | Where did I live? |

Where *did* I live?

I lived... in Montparnasse. Montparnasse, 269 rue St Jacques. La Rue St Jacques – beautiful – the seasons – the autumn – beautiful.

I lived like a bloody prince, you know. I'd walk all over.

In the mornings walk into college.

La Rue Saint Jacques on to Rue Gay Lussac.

Then across Le Boulevard Saint Michel.

Le Pantheon – magnificent building.

Dors bien Hugo,

Voltaire,

Rousseau.

You immortals.

Dormez bien!

|  |  |
|---|---|
|  | Hotel de Cluny, La Sorbonne. Fantastique! |
|  | Across to the Jardin du Luxembourg. |

*Rises to his feet – hanging light rises up with him*

|  |  |
|---|---|
|  | Old men playing boules. |
|  | Monsieur! Monsieur! |

*Music swells – lights come up*

|  |  |
|---|---|
|  | Balls! Balls! Balls! |
|  | I'd say hello to Charles. |

*RH looks up*

|  |  |
|---|---|
|  | Hello Monsieur Baudelaire? |
| RADIO | Bonjour. |
| RH | Ca va? |
| RADIO | Keep dreaming. It's a rule |
|  | No sage can dream such beauty as a fool. |
| RH | Too true. Too true. |
|  | The cafes! Ah the cafes! |
| RADIO | Qu' est ce-que vous voulez? |
| RH | Un cafe s'il vous plait. |

RADIO Voila.

RH Merci Madame.

Drink my coffee, watch the world, write a letter.

*RH puts on a red scarf*

RADIO Dear Father,

I have just started a magnificent abstract picture. This is clearly my forte. Don't be alarmed, one has to pass through this stage at one time or another.

Much Love

R

RH Was that meant to be me?

RADIO Yes.

RH Not bad.

RADIO Not bad.

RH Very good.

RADIO Very good.

RH Yes.

RADIO Yes.

RH And then on to the college.

*RH puts on a hat*

RADIO — Tout droit sur la Rue Vavin, a gauche sur la Rue Notre Dame des Champs et a gauche sur la Rue Joseph Bara.

Et tu seras arrive a l'Academie Ranson.

BOTH — Nous sommes arrives!

RH — Hello to the teacher.

Bonjour Monsieur Bissiere – Bonjour.

RADIO — Bonjour.

RH — He hardly said a bloody thing. Had an enormous nose like a great gannet.

Then on into the studio. Others all around.

Hopeless fools.

You fools.

RADIO — Fools!

RH — And enter the model for the day.

And today...

*RH stands on chair – looks out...*

...is May.

| | |
|---|---|
| RADIO | May! |
| RH | May. Enters – eyes on the floor – drifts between the easels – draped in a red coverture – a crimson gown – flowing behind – floor covered in paint – but not a spot on May. Not a spot. |
| | Perches on a wooden tabouret. Her throne. |
| RADIO | Magnifique! |
| RH | A moment. Waiting. |
| RADIO | Tick tock, tick tock. |
| RH | Then eyes up and around – up then down. Meet mine, meet mine! I'm here, meet mine. |
| | Never did. Not once. |
| | And then it's time. And with a round of the shoulders and an opening of the hands, the red blanket pours down from her body and bleeds in to the floor. |
| | She blushes a little – the red of the blanket now on her face – on her joues. |
| | The face, yes. The face. |
| | But the figure – the form – yes. |

Shoulders sweep – into arms. Hanging – heavy hands on lap.

Breasts – sitting – there – just there – nor up nor down – but there, you know – good tits.

Hips – les hanches. Delicate but the woman is there. She's there!

Cheveux. Yes aplenty. C'est bon, c'est bon.

Legs – foldered – neatly – slightly squeezed in sitting.

Why don't you stand for me? *Stand up.* Leve toi.

Come on May. *Stand!*

*Move* for me! You can move! Do it for me.

Your feet – your hands – your body – anything, anywhere, move!

Show me your shape.

You can May – you can – just stand – or step – or danse – or twist – saut – or stride – leap – or glide!

Move for me May.

Move.

Move.

Move.

*BEAT*

But she just sits.

A shame.

*Music fades – lights fade*

*RH steps off stool – walks back under the hanging light*

What a beautiful shame.

*He sits – light lowers*

Bit dramatic.

Too much don't you think?

Try and be sincere – don't try and make use of styles which are against your temperament.

*RH takes off hat and scarf*

*Lights cigarette*

You know what?

I am so fucking tired of Blue Peter.

Particularly that stupid woman Val.

I don't think that people who prostitute themselves in front of children, are good people.

I may have to exlude myself from the family when it's on so they can watch that execrable shit on their own.

My boys are the best in the world but what suits them doesn't suit me, you know?

It's the phoney falseness of it all – they're sort of magnified school teachers.

*BEAT*

Total cunts.

RADIO Well...

RH Quiet you.

*RH taps on the water jar*

RADIO Dance you beast, dance.

RH Listen to your inner voice. If you think of one thing, do something else.

RADIO There was an Old Man in a boat, Who said,

RH I'm afloat, I'm afloat!

| | |
|---|---|
| RADIO | When they said, |
| RH | No! You ain't! |
| RADIO | He was ready to faint. That unhappy Old Man in a boat. |

*RADIO and RH laugh*

*RADIO flashes*

*RH coughs*

*RH picks up painting – holds it to one side*

Never confront a painting face to face.

Same for your wife. Both are better seen out of the corner of the eye whilst you entertain yourself with lighter things.

*They both laugh*

*He notices whisky bottle*

*Holds it up*

Bloody hell! She's been at my whisky! How many times?

*Rings bell*

*Searches around the bed*

And where are my dill pickles?!

*Rings bell again*

I'm like one of those chicks waiting to be fed.

*Pours himself a whisky*

I've lost control – the reigns are no longer in my hands.

One thinks of Regan and Goneril and Lear.

Carry on Jeeves. Splash around.

Bugger it.

Lady bird, lady bird hurry back home,

My house is on fire and my family have flown.

*He drinks*

Oh yes.

*He reaches behind his bed*

Here you are.

*Lifts over a very large pickle jar – one pickle remaining – RH's face magnified through the water.*

I forgot about you, didn't I?

*Opens pickle jar – with difficulty*

*Picks up paint brush*

You'll do.

*Tries to stab pickle with the brush*

Don't play games with me/ come here/ right I've cornered you...

*Stabs the pickle*

Got you.

*Holds up pickle – skewered on paint brush*

*Makes to eat it*

No, I don't think I want it...

*Puts it back in the jar – puts down the jar*

Waste of bloody time.

You there?

*RADIO snores*

Oi!

*RH hits RADIO – flashes*

Wake up you snooze – box

RADIO Pillcock sat on Pillicock hill:

Halloo, halloo, loo, loo!

RH — Wake up you rotter.

RADIO — Sorry, sorry – it's very late.

RH — I know what time it is.

*Looks at watch – shakes it – listens to it*

Get myself a Hacker! They get all the stations.

RADIO — Not a Hacker!

RH — Yes a Hacker. There's a man in *St Just* – fixes radios – may have to send you there.

RADIO — Not St Just!

RH — Yes St Just!

RADIO — No – please.

RH — Yes – please.

RADIO — No.

RH — Yes.

RADIO — No.

RH — Well...

RADIO — Why do you live by the coast?

RH Well I say, you've made a fine recovery haven't you?

RADIO Thank you.

RH Keep it up.

RADIO Will do.

RH The coast.

Well some artists will say that it is the light and the space that draws them down to the coastline.

The open rugged landscapes.

The dramatic scenery.

Etcetera.

*BEAT*

Balls. It's good for the children and the houses are cheap.

I've got a 60 Watt bulb and I keep the curtains shut. Thank god I can enjoy it without needing to paint it.

*Lights cigarette*

The wives of the sailors would come to these cliffs to wave goodbye to their husbands. The sailors would appear like mice upon the decks. The women looked out as long as they could - until the boats dropped off the horizon.

*Holds picture up for RADIO*

What do you think of this?

RADIO That's lovely, lovely, really lovely...

What is it?

RH It's a crocodile

RADIO Right.

RH A crocodile – there... see?

See?

*BEAT*

It's eating my wife.

RADIO Ah yes, yes, yes.

RH Surely you can see it's a crocodile?

I'm not so good on crocodiles.

Music!

RADIO How about a story?

RH No – I'd like some music.

RADIO Right oh.

RH Galli Curci.

RADIO Galli Curci.

*Music – Galli Curci; Rigoletto*

*Lights change*

RH You can clearly see it's a crocodile – surely...

Look at it's jaws.

Clearly...

*RH opens mouth*

Of course it's a crocodile.

Waste of bloody time.

Bugger it – I've had enough.

I'll burst forth from this cell – mark my word.

*RH leans over his table and pulls over rope barrier*

And you can turn that bloody din off – don't know why I asked for that woman anyway – sounds like she's strangling herself with a pair of tights.

*Music gets louder*

RH No more.

RADIO Have you had enough?

RH No more. That's it. Ecouter.

RADIO But we haven't finished.

RH Not listening.

RADIO Is it something I said?

RH You're not listening.

RADIO Could you...

RH No. I don't know the words.

RADIO You do.

RH I don't.

Goat – tree – fart – barge – hick up.

See, haven't got a fucking clue.

RADIO But you were doing so well.

RH Oh, sod off you sycophant.

RADIO Well can you pick that up then please?

RH Kick against the pricks.

One has to kick and go on kicking.

RADIO Could you pick that up please.

RH No more words.

RADIO Pick that up please.

RH Are you deaf or dumb you blind fool? I'm not speaking anymore.

RADIO Yes you are.

RH I'm not.

RADIO You just did.

RH Well – from now.

RADIO Pick that up.

RH What is this? A bloody work camp? Haven't I got enough to do? I'm run off my feet. Look at me. I have work to do. This isn't a holiday. Now leave me alone.

Not another word!

*Hits RADIO – music stops – RADIO flashes*

*He goes back to his painting*

I will say one more thing.

Whoever called their son Darius was a fool.

*He paints*

RADIO — Pick it up.

Pick it up.

Pick it up.

Pick it up.

Pick it up.

Pick it up.

Pick it up.

RH — Alright, alright. I'll pick it up if it will keep you quiet. I thought you're batteries were running out.

Pick it up, pick it up. I'm picking it up.

*RH picks up rope barrier*

Here?

Here?

Or here?

*He slams it down*

No touching.

No feeding.

No fucking.

*BEAT*

Balls.

*He sits*

When you enter this world you are no longer a free agent – you can't move this way and that as the wind pleases. You are immediately in the machine, in a car park.

Not even your dreams are your own.

RADIO Would you like a story?

RH A story? I'll tell you a story.

Once upon a time I met Francis Bacon. I walked up to him and I told him what a bloody awful painter he was.

Which was absolutely true. He didn't have the first clue about painting.

He said he'd like to come around to my studio so I could teach him.

And he'd lend me some of his genius.

Bastard.

*RADIO laughs – glows*

Quiet you.

Question

RADIO What is your earliest memory?

RH Bloody hell – good one.

RADIO Thank you very much.

*BEAT*

RH There was one holiday I had as a young boy. I remember it as if it were yesterday. It was down the road – in *St Just*.

I took a wander down to the coast and I caught sight of this young Cornish girl – a local girl, you know. She was wearing a blue dress – Midnight Blue. Fantastic.

I remember it like it was yesterday.

RADIO Was she very pretty?

RH Not the girl – the dress – the blue – the blue.

I believe colours can be made to speak. I have a great belief in colour – a colour if good enough can stand on its own – irrespective of its shape. But they are influenced by each other. That's where the dicey part comes in, you know. I mean the balancing act.

I look at my colours and I believe they are living things. A colour can remain as alive and as fresh as the day it was painted.

*BEAT*

I can't remember the girl's face – but I remember the blue dress.

RADIO Did you speak to her?

RH Christ no – I was too scared. I think I followed her for a while. A bit frightening for her I expect. No when it came to talking to girls I came unstuck.

But the dress spoke.

RH I know – I was watching you.

RADIO What?

RADIO Would you like some music?

RH No – too much music is bad for an artist.

RADIO Question?

RH No more questions!

It's not so much what you put in but what you leave out – same in life.

RADIO Story time?

RH No I don't want a bedtime story.

RADIO How about a game?

*BEAT*

RH A game?

RADIO Something *fun.*

RH Something fun?

RADIO Yes – something fun.

How about hide and seek?

RH Good idea.

RADIO I'm full of them,

RH Aren't you just.

RADIO I'll hide you seek.

*BEAT*

RH No, I'm not sure that's going to work.

RADIO Okay, you hide I'll seek.

RH Right – okay – count to ten – and no peekaboo.

*RADIO counts to ten – RH makes to hide*

RADIO ...9 – 10.

*BEAT*

There you are – at the end of the bed.

RH Balls. Not enough time. Count to 10 again.

*RADIO counts to 10*

*RH looks for somewhere to hide – covers himself with a blanket at the end of bed*

RADIO ...9 – 10. Coming ready or not?

*BEAT*

You're under the blanket

RH Balls!!!

I haven't got enough time!

Count to 10 again.

And no sneaky peeks – I'm watching you.

*RADIO counts to 10*

*RH again looks for somewhere to hide. Spies the wardrobe*

*RH enters the wardrobe – closes doors*

RADIO ...9 – 10. Here I come... I'm coming to get you.

I will get you.

*BEAT*

But first I think it's time for a story.

Are we all sitting comfortably?

*BEAT*

Are we?

Are we though?

Good – then I'll begin.

*Lights fade down – RADIO lights up*

It's called The Dog Crusoe and His Master.

The dog Crusoe was once a pup. Now do not, courteous listener, toss your head contemptuously, and exclaim, "Of course he was; I could have told you that." You know very well that you have often seen a man above six feet high, broad and powerful as a lion, with a bronzed shaggy visage and the stern glance of an eagle, of whom you have said, or thought, or heard others say, “It is scarcely possible to believe that such a man was once a squalling baby.” If you had seen our hero in all the strength and majesty of full-grown doghood, you would have experienced a vague sort of surprise had we told you – as we now repeat – that the dog Crusoe was once a pup – a soft, round, sprawling, squeaking pup, as fat as a tallow candle, and as blind as a bat.

But I draw particular attention to the fact of Crusoe's having once been a pup, because in connection with the days of his puppyhood there hangs a tale.

This peculiar dog may thus be said to have had two tails – one in connection with his body, the other with his career. This tale, though short, is very harrowing…”

*The wardrobe doors fly open – lights up – RH falls face down on the floor*

RH I fell asleep...

*RADIO howls with laughter – flashes*

Shut up you!

The fun is over.

*More laughter*

Quiet.

*More laughter*

You've been reading stories haven't you.

*More laughter*

That's it – I'm taking you to St Just first thing in the morning.

*More laughter... laughter subsides... laughter turns into snoring...*

*RADIO snores*

Well that's just dandy, isn't it?

Well no more from me either.

Sod it.

*RH picks up pieces of paper from the floor – throws them around the room/audience*

*A piece of paper hits the wall*

*RH stops*

*RH goes over to wall – taps on the wall – listens – pushes the wall – the canvas gives...*

Yes of course.

*Looks down at rope barrier*

*Walks over to rope – puts foot over – lights go down – foot goes back – lights up – foot goes over – lights down – foot goes back – lights up*

Of course, of course, of course.

*He chuckles – moves around the room – looking – searching*

*He moves to the back wall – removes a painting from the wall – throws it over the flat – he looks out*

*Picks up some charcoal*

RH Paint as if you're painting a wall.

*Draws large female nude figure on the back wall*

*As he finishes the left foot…*

*Music from RADIO – Andrews Sisters; Bei Mir Bistu Shein*

*BEAR appears from wardrobe*

*Lights change*

*RH turns and sees BEAR*

*BEAR – menacing – turns toward RH – music builds – RH terrified…*

*Suddenly… they dance*

*Then close – intimate – BEAR holds RH – undoes RH's belt – trousers drop to floor – BEAR claws on RH's legs and thighs*

*BEAR slowly leaves through wardrobe – closes doors*

*Music stops – Lights change*

*RH pulls up trousers*

If your drawing is bad don't hope it will get better. Be certain on the contrary that it will get worse.

*Picks up paint brush – enters wardrobe – closes doors*

Where are you?

Where are you?

There you are...

Get out there – go on – move – move!

*BEAR appears through wardrobe – followed by RH*

Move you beast – sit down there – now sit there and shut up – I said be quiet!

*BEAR looks out at audience*

*RH prods at BEAR with paint brush*

Back! Back! Sit down there! Sit!

I said sit!

*BEAR sits down*

Right...

*RH drops paint brush. Gathers two books from the floor – gives one to BEAR*

Now you read Cordelia – no, I don't want complaints – you're Cordelia – you can't be Lear – I'm Lear – I'm Lear – now we'll start from the bit where she says... Are you paying attention? For God's sake shut up and concentrate! Now you begin... there.

Begin.

Commence.

*BEAT*

I can see this isn't going to work, is it?

Look, you can't be Lear. I'm Lear. *I'm Lear.* Don't you go all Prima Donna on me young lady. Now you do as you're told.

So I'll go from "So young, and so untender?"

Ready?

Good

So young, and so untender?

*BEAT*

You're sulking aren't you?

After all I've done for you...

Fucking princess.

*BEAT*

Do it for me – please.

*BEAT*

Sod it – I don't need you.

Come, let's away to prison:

We two alone will sing like birds I'the cage:

When thou dost ask me blessing, I'll kneel down,

And ask of thee forgiveness:

*RH slowly sits on the corner of the bed with his back to the audience*

So we'll live,

And pray, and sing, and tell old tales, and laugh

At gilded butterflies.

I am a very foolish fond old man,

Fourscore and upward, not an hour more nor less;

And, to deal plainly,

I fear I am not in my perfect mind.

*BEAR and RH look at each other*

*BEAR stands – towering above RH – BEAR raises it's paws towards RH – then tenderly begins to claw at his face – rips out a page of the book – rams it in to RH's mouth – drops the book – leaves through the wardrobe*

*Lights change*

*RADIO starts snoring*

RADIO Not St Just, just not St Just...

*RH sits back in his bed*

*RH hits RADIO – flashes*

Where am I?

RH I ask myself that same question every time I wake.

It can take me minutes before I realise where I am.

Sometimes hours.

I'm just left hanging, you know.

RADIO Suspended?

RH Yes, that's right.

I don't like sleeping because I don't like waking, you know.

It's all shit anyway.

And at the bottom of the whole stinking heap is the artist, who tries to keep some probity.

The true artist does not reside in some ivory tower, overlooking his glorious domain. He does not surround himself with sycophants who mix his muddy paint with their pricks or construct tributes of him out of sticky scrapings of his own self-importance. He does not need his arse pressed against the window and his balls on display.

No, he has failing electrical appliances, paper thin walls and cats drinking his water.

But he will carry on anyway... because... he must...

| | |
|---|---|
| | He will just carry on. |
| RADIO | Bob bob bobbing along. |

*RADIO sings "When the Red Red Robin..."*

*Hits RADIO – flashes*

| | |
|---|---|
| RADIO | Tell me something I don't know. Tell me – tell us. |
| | *BEAT* |
| RH | When I was... |
| RADIO | Go on. |
| RH | No, doesn't matter... |
| RADIO | When you were... |
| RH | Don't... |
| RADIO | When you were a *young boy*? |
| RH | Yes – well – when I was a child, just a boy, knee high, I would have this dream, the same dream night after night. |
| | A bird would appear and perch on the end of my bed, tilt it's head and stare at me, you know. |
| RADIO | Go on. |

| | |
|---|---|
| RH | It was a crow or a blackbird of some sort. A blackbird I think. It would fly in through the window, I would always keep the window open and it would perch on the end of my bed. It would keep me company – it would talk to me, you know. |
| RADIO | What did it say? |
| RH | It would squark. |
| RADIO | Sqwark? |
| RH | Yes. Sqwark. |
| RADIO | Sqwark. |
| RH | And it would peck at my toes. |
| RADIO | Go on. |
| RH | I tried to shoo it away. But it wouldn't budge. |
| RADIO | Peck peck peck. |
| RH | It would look at me, you know really look at me. As if it knew me. It understood me. And I could trust it. It was my friend. And I would see him every night when I closed my eyes. |

And then the sqwarking would stop and it would read me a poem.

It would read me a poem.

RADIO Do you remember the poem?

RH I don't know.

RADIO Try.

RH Really?

RADIO Yes – try.

*BEAT*

RH A blackbird sat on the cliffs one day, staring out to sea.

He wondered whether the tide was high and what to have for tea.

Then he opened his wings, began to sing, "A sailors life for me!"

And off he flew, to Timbuktu, and headed out to sea.

But after an hour, he lost his power and began drop in height,

The more he flapped, his energy sapped, he tried with all his might,

Up popped a boat, bobbing afloat, of which he just caught sight,

He landed on deck, with a scratch and a peck, and sailed off into the night.

RADIO Did he make it to Timbuktu?

RH I don't know. He never told me.

He might have done. I don't know. He never told me.

RADIO Maybe he sailed to the South of France?

RH Yes, the South of France, that would be nice wouldn't it?

The South of France.

Nice, St Tropez – maybe Antibes?

Sunshine – warm winds – cool colours...

Yes the South of France. Of course. Yes, that's where it went – all this time – I knew it. I knew it.

*RADIO cackles – flashes*

What?

*More laughs*

What are you laughing at?

*More laughs*

Be quiet...

Be quiet!

RADIO No – you quite!

You shhhh.

You listen.

You're not going anywhere.

What time is it?

RH What?

RADIO What time is it?

RH It's...

*RH looks at his watch.*

It's broken.

*It's broken.*

RADIO I haven't finished my story.

RH This is ridiculous – what story?

What do you mean?

What do you mean?!

*Ticking noises begins*

RADIO Poor Crusoe was singed almost naked. His wretched tail seemed little better than a piece of wire filed off to a point, and he vented his misery in piteous squeaks.

RH What?

RADIO The little dog put down its ears flat, and hung its head. "If you wish it I'll go away, sad and lonely, with my tail *very* much between my legs – indeed I will, only say the word, but – but I'd *rather* stay if I might."

*Storm noises begin – Black Bird poem is heard amongst the storm*

*Blue lights fade up*

RH I've had enough. Enough is enough.

No more.

I want this to stop.

I want this to stop...

Now!

Let me not be mad!

*Animal noises are heard*

Listen you fool – over I said – over!

I don't want to be part of this anymore - no more! I want no part in this jamboree!

*Rings bell*

No really I mean it – I really bloody mean it!

*Rings bell – rings – rings – rings… Noises swell…*

*He grabs hanging light – as if ripping it from the ceiling – holding it up like a search light over audience*

That's it!

Where are you?

*Searches with light*

Where are you?

Where are you?

What are you anyway? A bloody common burglar – a small time petty thief – sifting through dirty words and second hand pictures.

Where are you?

What?

You're all the same. You weatherman – you train driver – you factory worker – you pen-pusher! Do you really exist?

Wide eyed, open mouthed. Don't look at me. Do you stare at man making love or taking a shit? Do you?

Bugger off.

It's the artists who are the victims.

And not even an inquiring mind. *Your* minds and the journalists turning out their monthly paragraph.

You sit and watch and stare but you don't *see* anything do you?

Nothing.

Why don't you go and stand in front of a fucking mirror and have a good long look. What will you see?

Nothing.

Nothing will come of nothing!

Eyes shut, ears stuffed. Bloody dumb blind fools. You nothings!

*He stands on the bed – lights himself*

I am a Maker. I'll live on. I'll prosper. God stands up for bastards! I'll still be here.

On the walls and in the minds.

You nothings.

You're not even worth the dust which the rude wind blows in your face.

Fucking idiots!

*Throws light away – it swings back and forth*

*RH moves to wardrobe*

Go.

Goodbye.

Gone.

Abeintot.

Bon voyage!

*Enters wardrobe*

Art is essentially breaking out!

*Slams doors*

*Storm/ Animal noises stop*

*Doors open*

Balls!

*Closes doors*

*Music – Haydn; Die Schofung, Part II, "Mit Wurd" (The Creation)*

*Lights fade to black*

*Back-light up – illuminating the charcoal female nude on the back wall/ canvas. RH steps into light – silhouetted – paint brush in hand – pierces the nude with the brush – hand comes through – music swells – he rips canvas – he steps through – looks back – slowly walks back to bed.*

*Back-light fades out*

*Music fades*

*He sits on bed*

*Darkness*

*Hanging light slowly fades up*

*SILENCE*

*RH turns on radio – white noise*

*He turns it off*

Who is it can tell me who I am?

Breaking up or breaking down, going back or going on – it's all one process.

For me, my pictures stand for the hours I have passed with myself. The flashes of colour, the architecture of the lines, they are cries, calls, and attempts to stop for a moment the terrible march of destiny.

Painting a picture, kicking a ball, jumping in a puddle of mud.

You dredge up bits from the past – past lives, past women, past children – past paintings.

But the trappings are nothing, nothing. It is your internal life which counts. The outside things, the ephemera, are something to be fended off – like dogs, cats, chickens or fowls.

Don't try to make a successful drawing or painting. That is of no interest. Seek rather to learn something – to make that step forward – to find a purpose. Possess a discipline and a method which will save you from blindly searching in the dark.

Then, only then, can you live without danger. You can forget these instructions and trust to your own strength – your own sensibility. Because in the last resort it is the heart which says everything, and there I can no longer help.

*He looks down the bed*

I think sleep is a retreat. Perhaps a necessary one, but still a retreat.

*He pulls his legs back into bed*

A giving up, a back to the womb.

Necessary for the subconscious no doubt.

I shall now sleep.

*Makes to lie down – turns*

Faute de mieux.

*Makes to lie down – turns*

Well there's nothing better to do, you know.

*Lies down*

*Fade to black*

*VO*

Tell me the time. The time

Is Botallack O'clock.

This is the dead of night.

He switches the light on

To find a cigarette

*RH turns on hanging light – pours a whiskey – lights a cigarette*

And pours himself a Teachers.

He picks me up and holds me

Near his lonely face

To see my hands. He thinks

He is not being watched.

The images of his dreams

Are still about his face

As he spits and tries not

To remember where he was.

*Music – Sleepy Lagoon*

I am only a watch

And pray time hastes away

I think I am running down.

*Projections appear on to back wall – paintings/ letters/ a photograph of Roger*

*RH smokes – watches projections with audience*

*Final Projection*

*RH lies on to his back*

*Smokes*

*Fade to black – END*